P9-DIY-725

The Art of
Rubber Stamping

The Art of
Rubber Stamping

Suze Weinberg

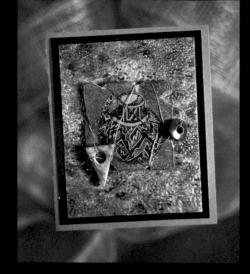

Library of Congress Cataloging-in-Publication Data Available

For Chapelle Limited
Owner: Jo Packham
Editor: Ann Bear

Staff: Marie Barber, Areta Bingham, Kass Burchett, Rebecca Christensen, Brenda Doncouse, Dana Durney, Marilyn Goff, Holly Hollingsworth, Susan Jorgensen, Barbara Milburn, Linda Orton, Karmen Quinney, Leslie Ridenour, Cindy Stoeckl, Gina Swapp

Photography: Kevin Dilley, Photographer for Hazen Photography
Photo styling: Brenda Doncouse

If you have any questions or comments, please contact:
Chapelle, Ltd.
P.O. Box 9252
Ogden, UT 84409

(801) 621-2777
Fax (801) 621-2788
chapelle1@aol.com

The written instructions, photographs, designs, and projects in this volume are intended for the personal use of the reader and may be reproduced for that purpose only. Any other use, especially commercial use, is forbidden under law without the written permission of the copyright holder.

Every effort has been made to ensure that all information in this book is accurate. However, due to differing conditions, tools, and individual skills, the publisher cannot be responsible for any injuries, losses, and/or other damages which may result from the use of the information in this book.

10   9   8   7   6   5   4   3   2   1

Published by Sterling Publishing Company, Inc.
387 Park Avenue South, New York, N.Y. 10016
© 2000 by Chapelle Limited
Distributed in Canada by Sterling Publishing
c/o Canadian Manda Group, One Atlantic Avenue, Suite 105
Toronto, Ontario, Canada M6K 3E7
Distributed in Great Britain and Europe by Cassell PLC
Wellington House, 125 Strand, London WC2R 0BB, England
Distributed in Australia by Capricorn Link (Australia) Pty Ltd.
P.O. Box 6651, Baulkham Hills, Business Centre, NSW 2153, Australia
Printed in China
All rights reserved

Sterling ISBN 0-8069-9976-4

Acknowledgments

Stamping has taken me all over the world. Sometimes, it's almost impossible to imagine the places I have seen. I have made so many wonderful friends and acquaintances who have taken my classes, shared their ideas and techniques with me freely, and supported me in so many ways. It is to those stampers everywhere, that I dedicate this book.

Very personal and special thanks go to Janine Ptaszynski and Michelle Paglino, who run my studio and keep me sane. To Annie and Vince at Ranger Industries, who believed in me from the very start. And, to my dear, wonderful husband Lenny, who has been a guiding force for 36 years and whom (I believe) is a secret stamper at heart!

About the Author

Nationally known rubber stamper Suze Weinberg has been designing and creating with rubber stamps for over 16 years. Suze is a former president of Jersey Shore Calligraphers Guild and has been a professional calligrapher for 17 years. She owns and operates the Suze Weinberg Design Studio, Inc., in Howell, N.J. Her calligraphic and stamped work has been published in the *Speedball Textbook*, *Greeting Card Design Book*, *Rubber Stamper Magazine*, *RubberStampMadness*, *National Stampagraphic*, *VAMP Stamp News*, *Calligraphy Review*, and her own book *Do It Yourself Calligraphy*.

For several years, Suze has been teaching rubber stamp classes for stamp stores, clubs, and conventions. She also holds calligraphy workshops for guilds and conferences all over the United States. She recently expanded her horizons to include teaching in Germany, England, South Africa, Australia, and two Royal Caribbean cruises.

Suze and husband Lenny have been married for 36 years. They have three children, three grandchildren, and four cats.

Forward

If you are ready to take your passion for stamping to the next level and are looking for a new creative challenge, you'll find many new and innovative techniques in this book—the kind of techniques that you'll use over and over again. They are easy to learn, yet produce sophisticated results.

New stamp designs, new surfaces, and new products are all necessary for rubber stampers to continue to enjoy their craft. I applaud the many manufacturers that invest in bringing these products to our market. But, it is the imaginative, passionate designers and teachers that keep stampers challenged. Through classes, demonstrations, magazines, and books, these talented people create and teach new techniques that serve as inspiration for us all.

Suze Weinberg is one of those designers. She has helped thousands of stampers explore their creative potential and has challenged every traditional stamping method and technique. I have worked closely with Suze for three years. Her boundless energy and enthusiasm for sharing techniques continues to amaze me. I know you'll be amazed when you see the results you can achieve with the techniques presented in this book.

I encourage you to jump in. Embrace new ideas. Try new surfaces. Get lost in your hobby and most of all, have fun.

Tammy Keck,
Publisher, Rubber Stamper Magazine

Table of Contents

I'll never forget my first stamping "encounter" some 18 years ago, a good friend sent me a birthday card, addressed in her finest calligraphy with five hand-carved rubber stamped apples decorating the bottom of the envelope. I can still remember my excitement! How did she get those apples to appear red and the stems and leaves green? And, whatever in the world was hand-carving?

When she explained that it all began with a carveable eraser, a knife, and some markers, it was all I could do to contain myself. And, when she explained that I, too, could make pretty images on paper even if I did not know how to carve or draw, I could not wait to hear how.

It was as simple as sending for some catalogs (barely a dollar each at that time) and ordering all the pretty inks and images I wanted. I cannot even remember how many one-dollar checks I wrote in the first month, but I'm sure it was obsessive!

Funnier still was the fact that I had not a clue in the world what I was supposed to do with all these pretty wooden-handled objects and colored ink pads that kept arriving weekly in my mailbox! But I experimented and, from those humble beginnings, began an adventure into Stampland far better than anything Alice experienced on her journey through Wonderland.

The beauty of those simple stamped apples on my birthday card has always stayed with me and is present whenever I sit down to create a stamped card or project. Keeping things simple, but at the same time exciting and interesting, has always been a challenge.

This book was, for me, another challenge. A way to express some of those simple concepts (things as easy as using household waxed paper or kitchen salt), yet to show them in ways unlike any others I had seen before. I discovered my niche, so to speak, as I sat down to experiment and soon realized that backgrounds and techniques were really more exciting to me than actually making a finished card project.

So, hopefully you'll agree that none of the projects or ideas I have presented in this book are too complicated to try. None of the cards are mounted on fancy papers or in a complicated way. Everything is kept to a minimum, yet, all of them are so adventurous that you will, hopefully, not want to stop, (especially once you have begun pulling out all the fun ingredients for cooking up your own stamped backgrounds.)

The trick is to relax and treat each project as a learning experience. I always say, it is not brain surgery, it's a card.

Everything has value. Days or weeks later, when you look at a project again, you may really like what you did not like when you first made it. If you simply enjoy the process, you are going to love the results!

General Instructions

Create beautiful backgrounds to accompany your rubber stamp projects with the *Art of Rubber Stamping*. Examples of the backgrounds are included with each set of technique instructions. Projects may be made following these instructions. Some background techniques may be applied to more than just traditional paper or card stock. Try them on different surfaces such as glass, plastic, or wood. Be certain to follow manufacturer's instructions and do not use any material that may damage the project or work surface. Some techniques may cause cards to curl, especially when sprayed with water. If card curls, place under a heavy book overnight to flatten.

Inks & Dyes

• **Dye and pigment powders** are colorants. They are mixed with a wide variety of bases including water, glycerin, wax, glycol, and various solvents.

• **Alcohol inks** come in a wide variety of colors and dry by evaporation. This type of ink was developed for artists and is not normally associated with rubber stamping. It can be found at fine art suppliers. Alcohol inks dry quickly and permanently and will stain skin, clothing, and rubber stamps. When working with alcohol inks, always work in a well-ventilated area, wear rubber gloves, and protect the work surface.

• **Archival inks** are water and fade resistant, pH neutral or acid free and nonsmear. They are made for paper and are the right choice for photo albums and journals.

• **Heat-set inks** are pigmented with a special base allowing them to remain wet until heat-set with a heat gun. They also may be dried overnight.

• **Textile inks** are specially formulated for use with fabrics. They are permanent and washable. The ink may be applied directly to stamp before it is used. These inks also are available in a dauber-type bottle that can be applied directly onto the stamp.

• **Water-based dye inks** are the most popular and easiest to use. They dry quickly even on glossy paper. They provide an artistic watercolor effect when stamped on paper. The ink is watery in consistency, transparent, and appears brighter when stamped than it does in the pad or bottle. The colors blend together easily, and bleed into one another in a rainbow pad, creating additional hues. Because dyes dissolve in solution, they actually penetrate the surface they are marking. This means though dyes are very water soluble, they may stain (especially red and purple tones). Dye inks have a tendency to fade unless specifically labeled as archival.

Water-based pigment inks are thick with a creamy consistency. This type of ink is slow drying, fade resistant, and embossable. All white and metallic inks are pigmented. Pigments are bold and bright opaque colors and can be likened to oil paints. Pigments do not dissolve in solution, instead they form a suspension. For this reason, they produce a film on the surface they are marking, rather than penetrating and staining it. Although they can be intermixed to create an infinite array of shades, this suspension does not allow them to bleed together when several colors are side by side in a rainbow stamp pad. The major drawback to pigment inks is a slow drying time. However, this can be used as an advantage for embossing. Be certain not to stack, send, or touch until the ink is thoroughly dry.

Additional Supplies

• **Acrylic brayers** are hard and smooth. Ink will not penetrate into textured depressions.

• **Adhesive foam dots** are a form of double-sided tape. When used, they give a three-dimensional quality to projects.

• **Art markers** make a dramatic effect that can be attained by diluting the pen colors with a little water from a paintbrush. The image is stamped on paper; color is added, then blended by diluting with water. Pen colors can also be blended on a palette with water before applying to the stamped design.

• **Blender pens** are used to blend two or more ink colors by coloring over the top of the colors. Blending gives designs a more realistic and dimensional quality. While blending colors on paper, it is important not to overwork the paper, as it may tear.

• **Double-sided tape** is sticky on both sides and available at most craft stores. It is best used with heavier papers. There are several varieties of double-sided tape.

Be certain to choose the heat-resistant variety with projects requiring heat-embossing or heat-set inks.

• **Double-sided heat-resistant adhesive sheets** are sticky and protected by liners on both sides. Large shapes may be cut from the sheets and may be more appropriate for mounting than double-sided tape.

• **Embossing powders** are available in many opaque colors as well as metallic, iridescent, and sparklers, which contain glitter. These powders are sprinkled over pigment ink and then heat-set, using a heat gun.

• **Heat guns** are made for embossing. They get very hot, but they do not blow much air.

• **Puff paint** is a form of fabric paint and is not normally associated with rubber stamping. It is generally used by fabric artists and crafters to make fuzzy teddy bears, Santa's beard, or other fabric appliqué projects. It comes in many colors and is found at most fabric stores.

- **Rubber stamps** are available in many sizes and are mounted on a wood or acrylic block, a piece of dense foam, or a roller. The images are basically of two types—a stencil-type solid image, or a line drawing. A well-made stamp will give a detailed and clean impression when stamped, regardless of a wood or foam mount. Along with picture stamps, include some word stamps in your collection.

- **Soft rubber brayers** are the most commonly used brayers for creating backgrounds. Ink the entire surface of the brayer by rolling it over solid or rainbow dye ink pads. Markers can also be used to color the soft rubber brayer. While holding the brayer upright with the end of its handle resting on a work surface, apply the markers to the rubber roller as it is turned.

- **Stamp pads** are generally made with dye or pigment ink in a water/glycerin/glycol base. Rainbow pads offer a fabulous blend of colors. Some of the dark colors used in rainbow pads tend to stain rubber stamps and brayers. The colors in pigment-based rainbow pads will not blend with each other, so they stay perfectly separated. One of their biggest advantages is that the slow-drying inks allow time to add embossing powders that need to be heat-set. Pigment inks may be used without powders only on porous paper. If used on glossy paper without powder, it will not dry.

- **A stylus** is basically a pencil-like tool with a blunt metal point on each end and comes in various sizes. It is used to score fold lines or to create texture.

- **Thick embossing enamel** is a large-particle resin that can be used in the same way as embossing powder, but is much more versatile and can create a smooth enamel-like surface. It also can be stamped after being heated with a heat gun, cracked for an aged look, or embellished.

Soft rubber brayers are a must for creating fabulous backgrounds.

Basic Stamping

1. Ink stamp with desired ink. Position stamp on a stamping surface and press firmly for several seconds. The larger the stamp, the more pressure should be applied.

2. When the stamped image is complete, clean the stamp thoroughly with a mixture of half water and half window cleaner sprayed on a clean rag or cleaning pad.

3. Dry stamp before applying more color.

Basic Embossing

Embossing transforms ink on a flat stamped image into a dimensional image by fusing finely grained clear or colored embossing powders to stamped image. Treating your surface with an antistatic pad will help eliminate unwanted specks on your finished project.

1. Ink stamp with embossing ink, then press on surface to be decorated.

2. Sprinkle embossing powder over wet ink. Shake off excess. A dry, fine paintbrush can be used to dust off any unwanted powder.

3. Heat powder until it melts, using a heat gun. Be certain not to over-heat project or powder.

Basic Brayering

Brayering softens colors used in a background. It spreads colors evenly over a surface, especially over a large area, and is good for applying color gradations.

1. Roll brayer over a stamp pad. Brayer may need to be rolled several times to coat it evenly.

2. Roll inked brayer over project to cover entire surface as desired.

Alcohol inks

No other ink interacts with glossy paper the way alcohol inks do. These inks are exquisite when they blend and meld together. However, they are also very permanent and can stain your hands and clothes. Be certain to wear a cover-up when you experiment with them. Gloves are a must or you'll be inventing a whole new manicure!

Supplies

Archival or heat-set ink pad

Assorted alcohol inks in refill bottles

Lightweight rubber gloves

Lint-free cotton cloth

Rubber stamp

White glossy card

Option: Fine-mist spray bottle with alcohol

Alcohol inks on a white glossy card can produce unusual and dramatic effects that resemble the cross section of a polished stone.

Squeeze several drops of color from assorted inks directly onto cotton cloth. Apply colors next to one another, overlapping slightly. Use enough ink to keep cotton wet but not dripping.

Press cotton cloth directly onto glossy paper. Press and daub color in an all over pattern, leaving no white space on card.

3. Option: While ink is still wet, spray ink sparingly with alcohol. Let dry.

Note: Patterns may be formed in the ink by spraying alcohol onto wet ink. Use caution, too much alcohol can ruin an otherwise perfect pattern and may dry splotchy as shown in photo. Alcohol inks dry on the surface almost immediately, but can leave a sticky residue if too much is used.

4. Stamp card with archival or heat-set ink.

Tips: Use one large stamp to cover entire card, or create unusual pieces with several smaller images.

These inks also look beautiful when used on other shiny or slick surfaces, such as metal and eggs (real or plastic).

3.

Alcohol inks may be combined with embellishments and other techniques. The card to the left combines thick embossing enamel with alcohol-ink stars adhered to the card with adhesive foam dots.

When stamping a large area, be certain to choose stamps with an open design which allows the polished stone appearance to show through.

Using alcohol ink is even more dramatic with this angel stamp. The image brings to mind stained glass cathedrals rather than polished stone. Cards such as this are perfect for Christmas, blessings, Christenings, or religious celebrations.

Thanks to Randall Curry of Michigan, I learned all about stamping on my photographs. It made me want to take pictures in an entirely new way and to look at my collection of rubber stamps in a completely different light.

Supplies

Archival or dye ink pad

Photographs of clouds or water (glossy or matte)

Scenic stamps

Spray fixative

Option: airbrush, sponges, or water-based markers

Note: Do not use a fabric or crafters type of ink as these inks require heat to set them and heating the surface will cause the emulsion on the photo to bubble.

Sky and water make excellent photographs for this technique. Other choices may include grass, flowerbeds, or treetops.

18

1. Stamp image directly onto photo with archival or dye ink. Let ink dry.

2.

2. Option: To add color, airbrush the photo, sponge on color, or apply color directly onto photo with water-based markers.

Note: Stencils also enhance the finished look, such as with the bright orange sun behind the Indian to the right.

3. Spray with fixative to retain sharpness.

On my magic carpet
my imagination will fly...
I'll stamp all the stars
and the clouds and the sky.

Several stamps were used together on this photo-stamping example. The addition of color to the cabin, woods, and sky give this card an aged and rustic look.

Here is a unique addition to stamping that can be found at most local fabric shops. Fusible webbing, used to iron two pieces of fabric together to create a permanent bond, can create a textural background when combined with rubber stamps for cards.

Supplies

Any color card (for background)

Archival or dye ink pad

Assorted colored fine embossing powders

Foam mounting tape

Fusible webbing

Heat gun

Rubber stamps

Scissors

White card (for stamped image)

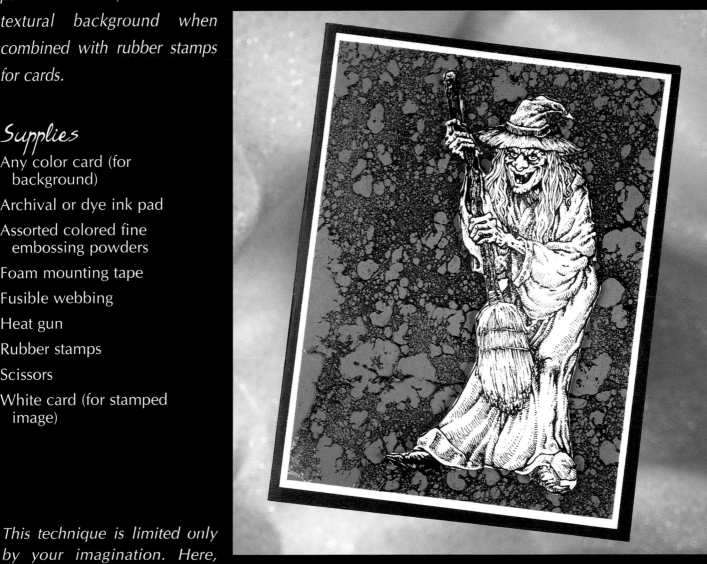

This technique is limited only by your imagination. Here, black embossing powder combines with fusible web on an

1. Cut a piece of webbing slightly larger than card. Lay webbing on top of card.

2. Heat webbing, using heat gun.

Note: Do not overheat. Use just enough heat to get webbing to adhere to the card surface. If any webbing overlaps the card, melt it away with heat gun or cut it away.

3. Apply embossing powders on webbing surface.

Note: This step may be done at any time, even days later. The powder will adhere to the surface, no ink is needed.

4. Reapply heat to melt powder.

Note: Webbing will separate further and adhere more to card.

5. Stamp (or stamp and heat-emboss) images with archival or dye ink onto separate card and cut out.

6. Adhere images onto surface with foam mounting tape to give it a raised appearance.

Several colors of embossing powders were added to the surface of this fusible webbing for a rainbow effect. One plain fish was cut in half and adhered to the card surface with craft glue. Two more fish were colored with markers and adhered over the cut fish with foam mounting tape for a dimensional school of fish.

In this example, a dark card was brayered with rainbow dye ink before the fusible web was applied to the card's surface. Gold embossing powder was applied to the fusible web. Embossing ink and gold powder were applied onto the butterfly image before adhering to the card with foam mounting tape.

Salt

Watercolor artists have long known the secret of salt. If you sprinkle salt onto wet paper that has been painted with watercolors, it produces a very unusual textural effect. For rubber stampers, dye-based inks react in a similar fashion. When applied to a glossy card, sprayed with water, and treated with salt, these, too, become like textured watercolors. I think you will love the results achieved from this very simple technique.

Supplies

Archival or heat-set ink pad

Fine-mist spray bottle with water

Gloss spray fixative

Household salt (table, kosher, rock)

Rainbow or solid-colored dye ink pad

Rubber stamp

Soft rubber brayer

White glossy card

Option: Embossing powder and heat gun

The weathered appearance caused by salt adds to the exotic beauty of this card. Hand-torn paper adhered to a background card with craft glue achieves a rough safari feel.

1. Brayer card with dye ink.

2. Spray card with water until dye ink colors run together.

3. Sprinkle wet card with salt.

Note: Do not sprinkle too much salt as it leaves areas looking dark and patchy.

4. Let salt dry thoroughly.

Note: Do not try to rush this process. As the salt dries, it will take on colors from the dye ink.

5. Brush off dried salt. Stamp card with archival or heat-set ink.

Tip: Brush the dry, colored salt into a plastic bag and save for use in a favorite shaker card.

6. Option: Heat-emboss card with embossing powder, using heat gun.

7. Spray card with fixative to retain sharpness of color and prevent fading.

Rainbow ink was brayered onto this card to create just the right mood.

This technique was applied to this die-cut to create a personalized frame and a unique card.

This background is perfect for stamps that depict movement such as these swimming fish.

Rock salt was used for this aquarium gravel "shaker card". After the card and salt dried, a ¼" foam frame was adhered to the card's surface with foam mounting tape. Clear plastic was adhered to the foam with foam mounting tape, enclosing the colored rock salt, which resembles aquarium gravel. A simple frame was cut from card stock and adhered onto the plastic with clear double-sided tape. Decorative border tape finishes this inventive card.

Waxed Paper

It was exciting to discover another use for waxed paper. I found I could produce dramatic resist effects when I transferred the wax to ordinary cards or paper, using an iron.

Supplies

Bond or typing paper

Gloss spray fixative

Iron and ironing board

Light-colored glossy or matte card

Rainbow or solid-colored dye ink pad

Rubber stamp

Scissors

Soft rubber brayer

Waxed paper

A dimensional effect is achieved on this card by using a die-cut machine, available for use at most craft and scrapbook suppliers, to cut this leaf from the background paper. A separate paper was stamped with similar leaves and sandwiched between the die-cut and background. As each layer was adhered to the next, glitter glue, embellished with holeless glass beads, was used to enhance the edges.

1. Cut waxed paper slightly larger than card. Crumple waxed paper into a ball.

Note: The more wrinkles in the waxed paper, the more detailed the pattern. Fewer wrinkles result in a broader pattern. Try folding your waxed paper origami-style for a unique and different pattern.

2. Open waxed paper and lay over card.

3. Place bond paper over waxed paper.

4. Press bond paper with iron on hottest setting, with no steam.

Note: Press for no more than five seconds. The wax will melt onto surface of both card and bond paper, and although invisible, will show up when you follow Step 5. If you press for too long, the wax will melt into the card and the technique will not work.

5. When cool enough to touch, remove waxed and bond papers.

6. Brayer both card and bond papers with dye ink to reveal waxed paper pattern.

Note: Ink will not fall into areas where there is wax. The wax acts as a resist. You may also brayer over the waxed paper to create yet a third texture.

7. Stamp image onto card with dye ink. Spray with fixative if desired.

Tip: You may also transfer wax to card by scribbling on a fresh piece of waxed paper with the prongs of a fork, as seen on the card below. A stencil, ballpoint pen tip (write messages), or any pointed object that makes lines may also be used.

A die-cut pop-up card was combined with the waxed paper technique to create this expressive card.

28

Waxed paper does not have to be discarded. Here, it is combined with a stamped embellishment to create this fabulous card.

I recall when I was learning calligraphy, my instructor taught me to use bleach in place of ink to create letters that would magically pop up on dark paper. I dipped a steel-nibbed pen into the bleach and wrote with it on a black linen card. The words came up like magic. This technique can be incorporated into stamping in much the same way.

Supplies

Chlorine bleach

Dark-colored matte card

Paper towels

Plastic plate

Rubber stamp

Scratch paper

Option: Soft rubber brayer and dye ink pad, markers, sponges

2.

1. Fold paper towels several times for thickness and lay on plastic plate. Pour enough bleach onto paper towels to be absorbed yet keep towel wet.

Note: Plastic plates help to keep the paper towels moist. A paper plate would absorb the bleach.

2. "Ink" rubber stamp with bleach from wet paper towels. Before pressing rubber stamp to card, gently blot off any excess bleach on scratch paper.

3. Stamp image onto card.

4. Options: Brayer rainbow or solid dye ink on a white card and "stamp" card with bleach.

Brayer the bleached area of a dark card with rainbow or solid dye ink after bleached area is dry.

To create a more abstract pattern, use a sponge to apply bleach to random areas.

4.

Plastic Wrap

Plastic wrap can turn an ordinary card into one that looks like frost on a windowpane. If you are patient and do not rush the drying process, you'll be amazed at the results.

Supplies

Archival or heat-set ink pad

Double-sided tape or foam mounting tape

Fine-mist spray bottle with water

Plastic wrap

Rainbow or solid-colored dye ink pad

Rubber stamp

Soft rubber brayer

White glossy card

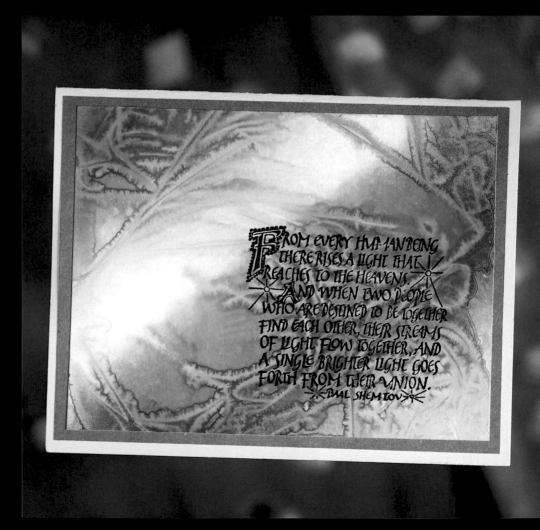

Blue ink helps to convey an especially frosty feel with this technique.

1. Brayer card with dye ink.

2. Spray card with water until color runs.

3. Place plastic wrap over wet card surface and scrunch plastic. Let it dry thoroughly.

4. When dry, carefully peel away plastic wrap.

5. Stamp image onto card with archival or heat-set ink. Let dry.

Note: Stamp onto separate paper and adhere with double-sided tape or foam mounting tape for a dimensional look.

Both subtle and dramatic effects can be achieved by manipulating the plastic wrap. More wrinkles will make a more frosted look. This card uses dramatic colors with subtle texture for a festive, jazzy card.

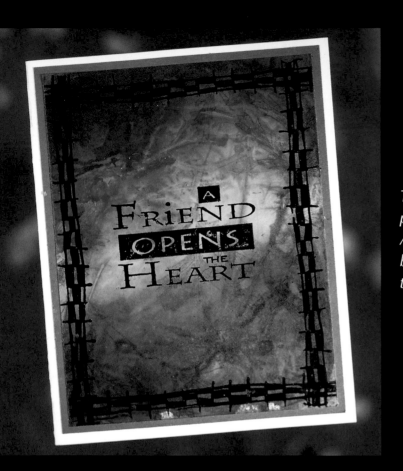

The texturized background created by the plastic wrap complements large open stamps. A plain card has been turned into a work of art by using color, hue, and space to emphasize text. The border pulls it all together.

The golden background and gold bar shape of this card is a basis to convey the value of true friendship.

This thin, loosely woven cotton cloth may be practical in the kitchen, but it is also perfect for creating dynamic backgrounds. It takes very little work and just a few supplies to get started.

Supplies

Cheesecloth

Double-sided tape or foam dot

Matte board approximately 8" x 8"

Packing tape

Rainbow or solid-colored dye ink pad

Rubber stamp

Scissors

Soft rubber brayer

White glossy card

1. Cut an 8" x 8" square of cheesecloth. Pull threads randomly from length and width of cheesecloth. Pull as many or as few as desired to make a loose and more abstract pattern.

2. Tape cheesecloth to three sides of matte board with packing tape.

3. Position card between cheesecloth and matte board as desired. Brayer ink over cheesecloth.

4. Rotate card. Brayer again with a different color ink. Repeat as desired.

5. Stamp image directly onto card or stamp image onto separate card. Cut out image. Adhere image onto card with double-sided tape or foam dot, or stamp directly onto background.

Multiple rainbow ink pads and just the right stamp create a psychedelic '60s feel with this card.

Above: The texture created by the cheesecloth in this background blends with the lattice framework border of the stamp. The colors are dusty and have a desert feel.

Left: The colors in this card are festive, in comparison with the colors in the card above. The grain of the cheesecloth texture combined with the gold embossing on the dancer's dress give an overall impression of fabric and festivity.

Brayer with Torn Paper

This is an easy technique that will instantly turn inexpensive bond paper and a plain card into a dramatic piece of art with a feeling of depth. Tear paper into freeform masks to create your own special look.

Supplies

Bond or typing paper

Rainbow or solid-colored dye ink pad

Repositionable glue or removable tape

Rubber stamp

Soft rubber brayer

White glossy or matte card

Even if you have never stamped before, this look is easily achieved. Beginners will have as much fun with it as the advanced stamper. It requires very few supplies and each card looks unique when finished.

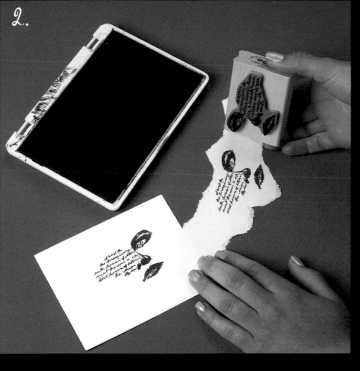

1. Stamp image onto card with dye ink.
2. Stamp same image onto bond or typing paper.
3. Tear around image on bond paper, creating a freeform mask.

4. Lay mask over stamped image on card, placing it approximately where stamped image is. Tack mask down with repositionable glue or removable tape.
5. Brayer over entire card with dye ink. Let ink dry, then remove mask.

Note: The effect is a feeling of depth within the white areas.

Torn paper com-
bined with this
stamp create a feel-
ing of depth and
looking at the world from the inside out. The color
frames the text, which seems to float in on a mist.

Masks can lay in any direction or be in any shape as shown in this vertical example. You may want to experiment with different shapes and positions for your mask and rubber stamp before completing your project.

For a different approach, you may try cutting interesting shapes to form the mask, such as this zigzag.

tissue papers that bleed or run when you wet them. Some inexpensive crepe papers may do the trick, too!

Supplies

Archival or heat-set ink pad

Fine-mist spray bottle with water

Noncolorfast art tissue paper (black, brown, or gray will not work for this)

Rubber stamp

White glossy card

"Confetti" is made on this card with a rubber stamp, but may also be made from several colors of markers dotted over the tissue paper color.

1. Tear tissue paper into abstract shapes and set aside.

2. Spray card with water until moderately wet.

3. Randomly, place colored tissue on wet card and spray with water to keep tissues wet.

Note: It is okay to have one color touching another. These colors bleed and form "tie-dye" patterns.

4. Let card with tissues dry thoroughly.

Note: The tissues will pop off when dry, leaving an abstract pattern on the card. To speed the process along, use a heat gun.

5. Stamp image onto card with archival or heat-set ink.

A stamp such as the one above, when combined with the Tissue Paper technique, provides many possibilities. With careful placement of the tissue paper, the hills could be left white for a snowy hillside, the sky could be made stormy by adding green, or a vivid sunset could be created by adding orange.

The look of this technique may be controlled by the amount of water used. The tissue paper on the card at the right was moistened moderately. The result is bright, bold colors that resemble blooming flowers.

The tissue paper on the card at the left was moistened excessively, allowing the color to run and feather. The result is a soft watercolor look.

Copy Mosaics

Thanks to the gals at Paper Parachute for showing me this technique. Combining a brayered background with colored tissue paper or real leaves from the garden can be spectacular, especially if you create a very attractive layout, then color copy it. This technique stamps directly onto the color copy.

Supplies

Any color dye ink, pigment ink or heat-set ink pad

Any color embossing powder

Clear-drying glue or double-sided tape

Colored tissue paper

Folded note card

Glossy card

Heat gun

Rainbow dye ink pad

Rubber stamp

Soft rubber brayer

There is no limit to the beautiful backgrounds you can create just by using your imagination and a color copier. Not only is the card flat and colorful, but you still have your original to use again.

1. Brayer rainbow ink onto glossy card.

2. Tear small pieces of colored tissue paper and tack onto card with a drop of glue. Leave some areas of the card free of tissue paper so you can see the brayered color.

Note: Be creative, if you want to use leaves from your backyard in place of colored tissue paper, tack them onto the card with double-sided tape.

3. Make a color copy of card.

4. Stamp image onto color copy with pigment or heat-set ink. Heat-emboss, using heat gun.

5. Adhere copy onto folded note card with glue or double-sided tape.

Stamping these ginkgo leaves over the center layer of this card could be tricky. But with a copy mosaic the stamping is done directly onto the copy.

Keeping a cache of extra color photocopies handy is a great way to make an instant card. The best stamps to use are those with an outline, so you can position the stamp exactly where you like the color best. For an exciting variation on this idea, color copy interesting backgrounds from maga-zine ads, or pieces of fabric.

my grandchildren. Had I pre
planned a little more carefully
and made them all the same size,
it could have been a book! Well,
there's always next time.

Supplies

Absorbent card (not glossy or
    matte finish)

Assorted colored inks, acrylic
    paints, or fabric dyes

Bond or typing paper

Heat-set or permanent ink

Newspaper or newsprint pad

Repositionable glue or
    removable tape

Rubber stamps

Scissors

Several fine-mist spray bottles
    for various color mediums

*Above and opposite: I thought it would be fun, at some point, to just
collect really large animal stamps. I never had any idea of what
I would do with them. When this novel idea came into my mind, I
spent an entire day stamping and spraying to see the different results.*

1. Stamp large image onto card with heat-set or permanent ink, using first stamp.

Note: Do not color image. The black and white final version will make a nice contrast to the colorful background you are about to create.

2. Fill individual fine-mist spray bottles with inks, diluted acrylic paints, or fabric dyes in assorted colors.

Note: Before beginning, feel free to experiment with how the different inks and dyes react together. Some paints will spatter, some will leave droplets of color, while others will form rings. The textures will all depend on the types of inks and paints used.

3. Stamp same image onto bond or typing paper. Cut out image, creating a mask. Lay mask over stamped image on card. Tack mask down with repositionable glue or removable tape.

4. Lay old newspaper or newsprint on floor. Place card on newspapers.

5. Stand back a few feet and spray card with dyes as desired.

6. Remove mask and let card dry thoroughly.

7. Any additional stamping may be done with heat-set or permanent ink when card is dry.

Marbled Metallic Markers

These wonderful markers are made from water-based pigments and will dry quickly and permanently on your card surface. For a short period of time after application, they can be reactivated by water and are extremely versatile for creating unusual and beautiful metallic backgrounds.

Supplies

Any dark color glossy card

Fine-mist spray bottle with water

Heat gun

Metallic markers

Rubber stamp

Scrap paper

Stamp cleaner

Option: Archival or heat-set ink pad, drinking straw, feather, sponge

Metallic markers have a luminous quality. This festive stamp is further enhanced by the electric blue background.

1. Spray card with water. Apply markers to card by scribbling, pressing, or dribbling until card is filled.

Note: These markers are a water-based, pigment ink and dry quickly and permanently. Depress marker on card surface to bring color to the tip. Scribble colors on card, or press harder and allow color to drip out from the tip. Using a few different colors will create beautiful marbled effects.

2. Spray the card with water again to move the color around on your card.

3. Option: For different effects, blow colors around with a straw, move them around with a feather, blot them with a sponge, or tip card from side to side by hand. Let dry.

Note: Moving the ink and drying may be done quickly, using a heat gun, but air drying is preferred.

Tip: Because these markers are water-based, they will not damage rubber stamps. Try applying metallic ink directly to the surface of the rubber stamp. This ink tends to go on a little heavy, so gently blot off excess ink on scrap paper before pressing stamp on card.

4. Stamp image onto card with metallic marker.

5. Option: Stamp image onto card with archival or heat-set ink.

6. Clean stamp immediately with stamp cleaner or water.

Dimension is created here in two ways, by embossing and the use of adhesive foam dots.

Here, the same color is used for both background and foreground by quartering and separating the background.

Texture was created on this card by pouncing a feather on the wet metallic marker surface. The giraffe stamp was heat-embossed, using a heat gun, and mounted with adhesive foam dots on black card stock.

Metallic markers were applied directly onto card on the bottom layer of this card and directly onto a leaf rubber stamp on the top layer. The leaf was stamped onto black glossy card stock.

By layering and framing, three different looks are used to enhance a single leaf image.

53

Metallic Markers with Brayer

I really enjoy working with these metallic markers because they offer so much versatility. You may mix and match them with other rubber stamping supplies to create unusual backgrounds. Here is a technique for using these markers in combination with a soft rubber brayer.

Supplies

Archival or heat-set ink pad

Fine-mist spray bottle with water

Metallic markers

Rubber stamp

Soft rubber brayer

White glossy card

Metallic markers are available in a wide variety of colors. Combined with this technique they can create amazing effects, such as this tropical sunset.

1. Spray brayer lightly.

2. Apply marker directly onto brayer surface by drawing lines or allowing ink to drip from the tip. Turn brayer as you apply so colors blend together like a kaleidoscope. Keep brayer lightly sprayed.

3. Brayer onto glossy card. Let dry.

4. Stamp image onto card with archival or heat-set ink.

Note: A silhouette stamp or one that is scenic in nature will help to set off the unusual background.

This stamp combined with soft pastel pink and blue metallic markers give the feel of a morning sunrise.

55

Supplies

Archival or heat-set ink

Fine-mist spray bottle
  with water

Metallic markers

Rainbow dye ink pad

Rubber stamp

Soft rubber brayer

White glossy card

A bold ink pad and metallic markers lend a tropical flare to this card.

1. Roll brayer over a well-inked rainbow dye ink pad. Roll back and forth until brayer is heavily loaded with color.

2. Spray brayer with water, turning brayer as you spray.

Note: The ink will move around, forming patterns.

3. Scribble metallic colors over rainbow ink on brayer. Keep brayer lightly sprayed.

4. Roll brayer on card.

5. Stamp image onto card with archival or heat-set ink.

An autumn ink pad combined with metallic markers give the look of a sunset when used with this stamp.

Metallic Marker with Dye Refill ink & Brayer

Trying different variations leads to new and exciting techniques. Here the addition of random drops of ink from a refill bottle adds spectacular splashes of color.

Supplies

Archival or heat-set ink pad

Assorted colored dye inks in refill bottles

Fine-mist spray bottle with water

Metallic markers

Rubber stamp

Soft rubber brayer

White glossy card

Decorative-edged scissors can add an artistic element to any card. In this example, the card was simply cut in half before mounting to the background card.

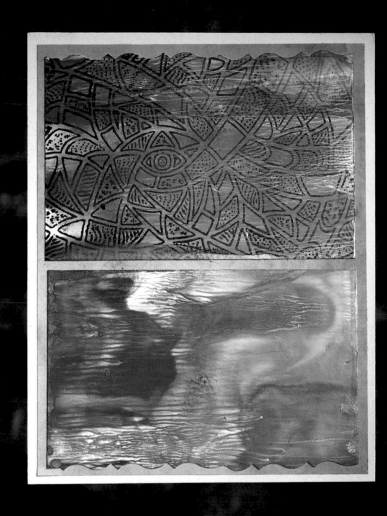

2. Apply metallic markers on wet brayer.

Note: Be certain to keep brayer lightly sprayed.

3. Drop small droplets of assorted dye ink colors from refill bottles over the wet metallic marker, turning brayer as you drop.

Note: Do this sparingly. Too much ink will take away from the final result.

4. Roll brayer onto card. Let dry.

5. Stamp image onto card with archival or heat-set ink.

In this example, the card is mounted on its background with the decorative edge facing out. The unstamped background could be used to write your own heartfelt message.

Metallic Markers & Plastic Wrap

Supplies

Archival or heat-set ink

Assorted colored metallic markers

Black glossy card

Fine-mist spray bottle with water

Plastic wrap

Rubber stamp

Metallic markers may be used on any color card, but dark cards set off the color and shimmer very dramatically. In this example, a smokey effect is achieved,

1. Apply metallic markers on card.

2. Spray card with water until color runs.

3. Place plastic wrap over wet surface and scrunch plastic wrap. Let dry thoroughly.

Note: If you let it air-dry, the surface should be flat enough to stamp. For a more heightened texture, let card dry under a warm lamp, but be careful not to burn the card. The heat will not only dry the card, but create even more heightened texture by causing the plastic wrap to adhere onto the card surface.

4. When dry, carefully peel away plastic wrap.

5. Stamp card with archival or heat-set ink. Let dry.

Above: If the card is too textural for direct stamping, stamp onto separate paper and adhere with double-sided tape or foam mounting tape for a dimensional look.

Left: Your choice of colors helps determine whether the textural effect is subtle or bold.

Liquid puff paint is a fabric paint that has a puffing agent in it. In stamping, it is used to make small puffy flowers, to fill in Santa's beard, or to make fuzzy teddy bears. Little did we realize that it could create amazing faux-leather finishes on cards.

Supplies

Assorted colored liquid puff paints

Any color matte or regular finish card (not glossy)

Archival or dye ink pad

Cosmetic sponge

Freezer wrap or waxed paper

Heat gun

Rubber stamp

Soft rubber brayer

Stamp cleaner

When creating faux leather, it is best to stick with traditional colors for leather, such as this maroon card. Other colors may include black, brown, tan, and rust.

1. Squeeze a few colors of liquid puff paint onto waxy surface of freezer wrap or waxed paper.

Note: Squeeze colors near one another.

2. Roll brayer into the liquid puff paint to smooth out and mix colors together.

Note: Roller should be well coated.

3. Brayer liquid puff paint onto card. Clean brayer immediately.

4. Heat liquid puff paint on card, using heat gun.

Note: No need to wait. As it dries, liquid puff paint begins to look like suede leather.

5. Stamp image onto card with archival or dye ink.

Note: You may also stamp onto the suede surface with a different color of liquid puff paint by applying it directly on your rubber stamp. Squeeze liquid puff paint on freezer paper or waxed paper. Choose a different color than those used on the card. Use a cosmetic sponge to lift liquid puff paint off of the freezer paper and pat it onto surface of the rubber stamp. Press stamp onto faux-leather surface and heat. The image will be raised.

6. Clean stamp immediately.

Note: If this product adheres to your rubber stamp or brayer it can ruin the surface.

Tips: Do not emboss newly stamped image. The embossing powder will adhere to the entire surface, not just a selective area.

Use decorative punches on freezer paper. This creates a stencil. Place freezer paper stencil on faux-leather card surface and sponge liquid puff paint through it. Heat-emboss, using heat gun.

The subtle suede look of this card and poetic stamp complement each other perfectly.

This "leather-on-leather" caveman look is very dramatic. It appears as the stamp was actually drawn on a stretched piece of leather.

These flowers were stamped with white and green puff paint applied directly to the rubber stamp. Holeless beads and glitter were added for a very unique look.

some Things have to be believed to be seen!

Suze Weinberg '97

This card uses a nontraditional color for leather. The green gives this card a mossy feel that may be desirable. The text was stamped directly onto the faux-leather surface and the pots were stamped separately and adhered onto the card with adhesive foam dots for a dimensional effect.

Spray Webbing

Spray webbing is a type of spray adhesive. It comes in assorted colors, both solid and metallic. Because of its sticky nature we can add exciting things to its surface as long as we work quickly.

Supplies

Any color card for stamping

Any color spray webbing

Dark-colored glossy or matte card for spray webbing

Double-sided heat-resistant adhesive sheet or adhesive foam dots

Rubber stamp

Scissors

Sheet of foil

Option: Assorted colored embossing powders

Gold and white spray webbing on a black matte card are the foundation for this beautiful card. All layers were mounted with double-sided adhesive sheets.

1. Place dark-colored card on a flat surface in a well-ventilated area. Spray webbing from 12" away, allowing it to waft to the card surface.

Note: This makes a beautiful finish and may be left just the way it is if desired.

2. For a more dramatic effect, foil may be added to web texture. Place foil (colored side up) on card surface. Let foil sit for a few minutes, then lift.

Note: The webbing will dry very quickly. There are only a few seconds after spraying to place foil on card surface. Some foil will transfer onto the webbing, leaving a shimmering effect.

3. Option: If you like added texture, lightly respray webbing over project and quickly apply embossing powder. Heat-emboss, using heat gun. Do not overheat or the foil underneath will melt away.

4. Stamp image onto separate card. Cut out stamped images and adhere onto card with double-sided heat-resistant adhesive sheets or adhesive foam dots.

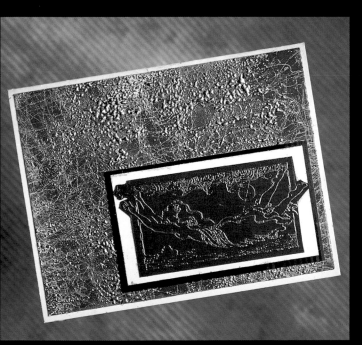

Gold embossing powder was added over the spray webbing on this card and heat-embossed.

Rainbow ink was brayered over white card stock to create this colorful card. Gold foil was applied on the bottom layer and silver foil on the heart.

Moldable Foam

This material can be found in sheets or blocks and is also available in assorted shapes. Prior to using for stamping, moldable foam was found primarily in toy stores where children bought it to play with in the bathtub. The beauty of this foam is that once heated with a heat gun, it can be pressed into anything textural, then inked and stamped. Heat it again to erase your design and reuse it by repeating the same process.

68

Supplies

Archival or heat-set ink pad

Glue gun with glue sticks

Heat gun

Matte board

Moldable foam block

Rainbow or solid dye ink pad

Soft rubber brayer

White glossy or matte card

This card was brayered with yellow dye ink and stamped with brown archival ink. The result is a beautiful flame-like appearance.

1. Brayer card with rainbow or solid dye ink . Let dry.

2. Randomly drizzle hot glue onto matte board, using a glue gun, creating a textural pattern. Let glue cool.

3. Heat surface of moldable foam block for about 30 seconds by moving heat gun over it in a circular motion. Avoid overheating any one spot.

4. Quickly press heated foam block against textural glue pattern. Hold down firmly for about 15 seconds.

Note: Moldable foam blocks can be pressed into any object or dimensional surface that has a texture. This might include things like a cluster of rubber bands, buttons, safety pins, a piece of lace, rice grains, netting, a wicker basket, or even crumpled paper. It can also include rubber stamps, which make very deep impressions when molded.

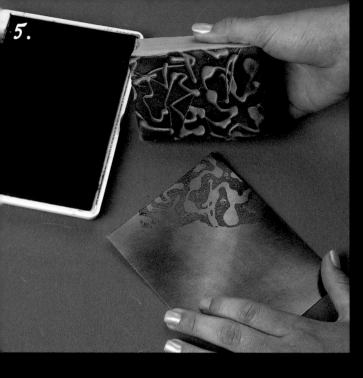

5. Ink foam block with either archival or heat-set ink. Press inked foam block on card to create an all-over pattern.

Note: Keep foam block well inked as you create this design. Varying degrees of pressure produce different results. Moldable foam may be cleaned with rubber stamp cleaner after use.

The foam-stamped background was combined here with a separate heart stamp and embossed message on white card stock.

After stamping with moldable foam, the text on this card was heat-embossed, using a heat gun, and embellished with holeless beads and iridescent glitter.

The card stamped with moldable foam serves as a foundation for this card and provides a colorful contrast to the black-and-white sun stamp.

Pearlized Dry Pigment Powders & Embossing Ink Resist

This beautiful technique produces a soft lustrous finish on your dark cards. It is a unique way to experiment with embossing ink and mica powders instead of embossing powder.

Supplies

Dark-colored matte card

Embossing ink pad or clear resist pad

Facial tissue

Pearlized dry pigment powders

Rubber stamp

Soft flat brush

Spray fixative

Decorative-edged corner scissors were used on this card to support the classic shape of the feather stamp. The soft golden glow comes from the application of dry pearlized pigment powders sitting on top of resist ink.

1. Stamp image onto card with embossing ink or clear resist ink.

Note: Be certain to make a good strong impression since image will not be visible on the dark card.

2. Pick up pearlized powder from jar, using soft flat brush.

3. Lightly brush powder onto inked image.

Note: Use more than one color if desired. No heating is necessary as this is not an embossing project.

4. Gently wipe over image with a facial tissue to remove excess powder.

5. Spray card with fixative to retain sharpness and to prevent embossing ink from evaporating.

Above: The word "Aspire" was embossed with clear embossing ink for a watery effect. The flying person was stamped separately on white card stock and adhered onto the background with an adhesive foam dot for dimension. The end result conveys a feeling of triumph over adversity.

Left: A large stamp was used here to create an entire host of butterflies to frame this single gold-embossed butterfly.

Brayer Resist with Embossing Ink

Here is a beautiful way to create a soft wallpaper-print background that takes little effort and is almost foolproof.

Supplies

Clear embossing ink pad or clear resist pad

Heat gun

Rainbow or solid-colored dye ink pad

Rubber stamp

Soft rubber brayer

Soft tissue

Spray fixative

White matte card

The clear embossing ink in this example creates a negative image. This effect, combined with just the right color of dye ink make for a nostalgic, sepia-toned appearance.

2. Let image air-dry for a few minutes or speed along with a heat gun. Image may remain somewhat damp.

3. Ink brayer thoroughly with rainbow or solid dye ink.

4. Brayer over image, going over it as many times as is necessary to produce a rich, even color.

Note: The stamped image will magically appear ghost-like under the brayer color, almost like a wallpaper print.

5. Wipe excess dye ink from surface, using soft facial tissue.

6. Spray card with fixative to retain sharpness and to prevent embossing ink from evaporating.

Note: Embossing ink that is not spray sealed may break down over time and disintegrate.

Soft foliage appears to be in this vase. The vase was stamped separately and adhered onto the card with an adhesive foam dot.

Stamps may be used to create frames around a centered image. In this example, the Kokopelli stamp was used multiple times to create both a frame and the central image.

In this example, multiple word stamps were used as a frame. Word stamps help to evoke emotion and convey ideas.

Hidden Color Embossing Resist

Reminiscent of a classic children's project that uses India ink and crayons, this resist technique uses embossing, markers, and dye ink. The results are simply beautiful.

Supplies

Antistatic pad

Assorted colored water-based markers or rainbow dye ink pad

Black water-based marker or black dye ink pad

Clear embossing ink pad or clear resist pad

Embossing powder

Facial tissue or soft cloth

Heat gun

Rubber stamp

Soft rubber brayer

White glossy card

A rainbow ink pad containing fall colors is perfect for this leafy card.

1. Scribble assorted markers over entire card surface. Let dry thoroughly.

Note: Keep the colors light and bright. A brayer with rainbow ink may be used instead.

2. Treat paper with antistatic pad to eliminate moisture and static.

3. Stamp image onto card with embossing ink or clear resist ink. Apply embossing powder. Heat-set, using heat gun.

4. Completely cover entire card with black marker or dye ink. Let card dry.

Note: The card should now be totally black.

5. Wipe embossed areas with facial tissue or soft cloth to expose color underneath.

Above: Adding stickers to your finished design can enhance a rubber stamp project, such as in this example.

Left: Here, a rainbow of colors shows through the spidery webbing of leaves.

Brayer Resist with Archival ink

Being able to see a light-colored ink under a dark background would seem impossible if it were not for this interesting way of mixing two non-compatible inks together to create a multitone resist effect.

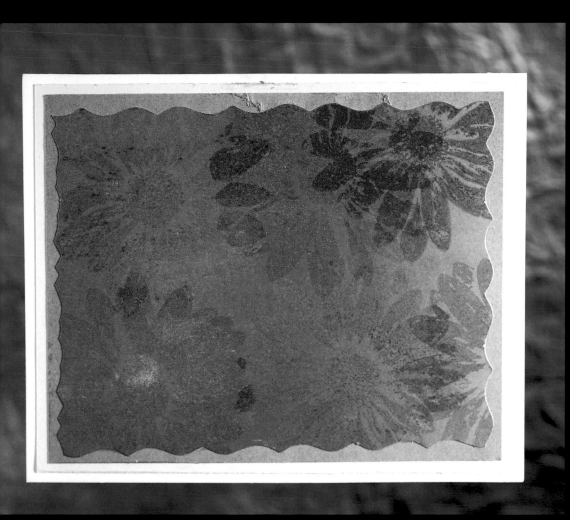

Supplies

Assorted colored archival
  ink pads

Facial tissue or soft cloth

Rainbow and solid-
  colored dye ink pads

Rubber stamp

Soft rubber brayer

White glossy card

Contrasting inks of light and dark were used here to create shadows and highlights on this card.

1. Stamp image onto card with archival ink. Let ink dry thoroughly, or speed along with heat gun.

Note: Stamp with light-colored archival ink, like yellow or pink, or use a very dark colored ink like black or olive green.

2. Brayer over stamped image with dye ink.

Note: The image will not smear. If you stamped with a light color, try using a darker color to go over it and vice versa. Rainbow inks produce beautiful results.

3. Wipe card surface with facial tissue or soft cloth to remove excess dye ink.

Note: This will help to brighten the underlying images.

4. Option: Stamp on top of finished card with archival or permanent ink.

Above: Many color combinations can be achieved with this technique.

Left: The lined texture on this card was created by wrapping rubber bands on the brayer before brayering archival ink onto card.

ink Pad Color with Blender

Blender pens offer a beautiful way to apply soft dry pigment color into a specific stamped area, creating glowing effects that stay permanently on your card surface with no need for spraying.

Supplies

Absorbent light-colored card
(not glossy or matte)

Blender pen

Rainbow dye ink pad

Rubber stamp with heavy
detail lines

Blender pens allow you to control color in between lined areas and create a softer color than traditional markers when filling in stamps.

1. Stamp image onto card with dye ink.

2. Rub over stamped image with blender pen tip.

Note: The colors will fill in like watercolors. For more intense color, you may apply the tip of the blender pen directly to the ink pad and pick up that color to apply to card.

3. Wipe blender pen clean on a towel or soft cloth.

An effect similar to a pastel wash is created in the example above by running the pen over the entire surface of the card.

Blending the colors in this collage stamp adds to the beauty and helps pull all the images

Painting with Blender Pen & Dry Pigment Powders

Supplies

- Assorted colored pearlized dry pigment powder
- Blender pen
- Clear embossing powder
- Dark-colored matte card
- Embossing, heat-set, or pigment ink pad
- Heat gun
- Paper plate or waxed paper
- Rubber stamp with an open design
- Towel or soft cloth
- Option: Spray fixative

This technique uses an embossed surface to help contain the color. The blender pen with dry pigment powder creates smooth, blended color.

1. Stamp image onto card with heat-set or pigment ink. Apply clear embossing powder on image. Heat-emboss image, using heat gun.

Note: Gold embossing powder is a nice alternative.

2. Tap a small amount of pigment powder onto a paper plate or piece of waxed paper. Pick up pigment powder, using tip of blender pen.

3. Fill in open areas of stamped design with pigment powder, using blender pen.

4. Wipe blender pen clean on towel or soft cloth when you want to change colors. Reapply as desired.

Note: The preservative in the blender pen seals in the dry pigment, making spray fixative optional.

5. Option: Spray card with fixative.

Corrugated paper adds to the beauty of this card. Embellishments, such as this heart, can be made from something as simple as cardboard and thick embossing enamel.

This mosaic stamp is further enhanced by using many colors of pigment powder. The card is embellished with an embossed image of the same stamp wrapped with wire and beads.

Create contrasting areas of light and dark by highlighting the background as shown here between the butterflies.

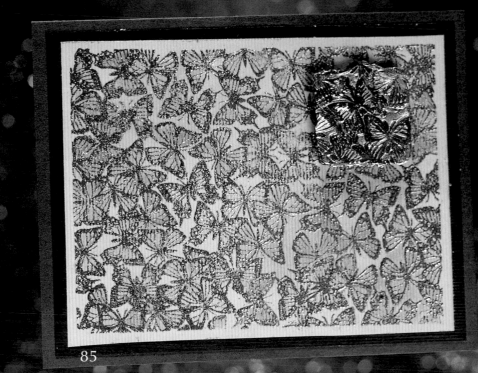

Embellishing with Glitter Glue

You do not always have to color in your stamped image with markers or colored pencils. Sometimes it is more interesting to fill in the open areas with dimensional products like colored glitter glue. In addition to paper, you may want to try the same technique on wooden eggs, boxes, or picture frames.

Supplies

Assorted colored glitter glues

Heat-set or pigment ink pad

Rubber stamps with an open image (not solid)

White glossy card

Option: Card for stamping, embossing powder and heat gun

Leaving selected areas of the image unfilled actually highlights this card. The white areas appear to be white enamel.

1. Option: Stamp image onto card or other surface with either heat-set or pigment ink.

2. Option: If using pigment ink, heat-emboss image with embossing powder, using heat gun as desired.

3. Fill in open areas or areas surrounding image with different colors of glitter glue. Let card dry overnight.

Note: Because glitter glue is a wet medium, your card may curl slightly. In the morning, glue will appear raised and brilliant in color, like jewels.

The beautiful shimmering effects on this project and those on page 88 were done with droplets of different colored glitter glues applied next to each other and allowed to dry. Expand your creativity by using other mediums. In addition to glitter glues, fill in open areas with pearlized craft paint, dimensional fabric paint, and glass beads.

Create more than just cards and frames. Papier maché and unfinished wooden boxes are available at local craft stores in many shapes and sizes.

Unusual items such as this egg make wonderful projects. The egg was randomly decorated and not stamped. However, eggs and other odd-shaped items may also be stamped before applying glitter glue.

Paper Gilding

Here is another simple and beautifully effective technique that requires no special skills and produces a gilded effect on ordinary paper bags.

Supplies

Acrylic brayer

Archival or dye ink pad

Brown craft paper, grocery bag, or optional papers as listed below

Double-sided tape

Embossing, heat-set, or pigment ink pad

Embossing powder

Folded note card

Heat gun

Rubber stamp

Scissors

Optional papers: Decorative wrapping paper, corrugated, lava, mulberry, banana, wallpaper, or any raised surface.

Choose paper that will complement the color of the embossing powder. The powder will highlight only the raised areas, leaving the paper color to show through.

Multiple colors of embossing powder were used on this card. The simple black-and-white stamp complements this colorful, nubby background.

1. Cut craft paper or bag to desired card size.

Note: Stamp image onto paper with archival or dye ink, if desired.

2. Crumple paper and open.

Note: Eliminate this step if your paper already has a raised texture. Use this same approach on the optional papers listed on page 89 if they do not already have a raised surface.

3. Brayer over paper with embossing, heat-set, or pigment ink, using acrylic brayer.

Note: The ink will settle only on the raised areas. The acrylic brayer may be rolled up and down, side to side, or even around in circles. A soft rubber brayer will not work as well for this technique as the ink will want to settle in unwanted areas.

4. Apply embossing powder on wet surface. Heat-emboss, using heat gun.

5. Adhere paper onto card with double-sided tape.

6. Stamp image onto separate paper with archival or dye ink. Cut out stamped image.

7. Adhere onto card with double-sided tape.

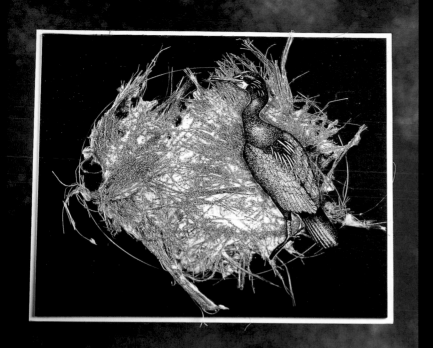

This beautiful hand-made paper from South Africa is richly textural and lends itself beautifully to this technique. Hand-made papers do not have a grain and, when torn, will produce a marvelous jagged line in any direction. The end result depends on how fibrous the paper is. The more fibrous the paper, the more jagged the tear.

In this example, black embossing powder is striking on red paper. Imagine the opposite, a sparkling embossing powder over black paper. Paper gilding is virtually mistake-proof for creating textured backgrounds.

Adhesive Sheets & Fabric Lace

Some double-sided adhesive sheets are heat-resistant. These sheets are very sticky and protected by liners on both sides. They do not yellow and are considered archival, making them great for use in scrapbooks and the like. But they are even more fabulous when you adhere things onto them, because they will not lift off.

Supplies

Antistatic pad

Bone folder

Double-sided heat-resistant
   adhesive sheet

Fabric lace

Fine glitter

Glass beads with no holes

Large plastic zip-top bag

Matte board or heavy card

Scissors

Scrap paper

With this technique we used a double-sided adhesive sheet to create some very unusual and permanent lace pattern backgrounds. You'll be a-mazed because this technique uses no ink and no rubber stamps. Rubber stamping may be done separately, such as the cards on pages 94–95.

1. Cut adhesive sheet to same size as matte board or card. Pull liner off of one side of sheet and adhere to board. Pull second liner off sheet.

2. Cut fabric lace slightly larger than matte board or card. Adhere lace onto adhesive sheet. Flatten lace well, using a bone folder.

3. Sprinkle loose glitter over lace. It will adhere to the exposed areas of the sheet.

4. Before returning excess glitter to bottle, use antistatic pad on a piece of scrap paper to demagnetize it. Tap excess glitter onto scrap paper, then return glitter to jar.

5. Carefully pull lace from adhesive sheet.

Note: Lace will lift easily and whatever areas of the pattern the glitter did not adhere to will be left sticky.

6. Pour glass beads into plastic bag and insert card. Seal bag and shake.

Note: All remaining areas will fill with beads, finishing off your design. Your original piece of lace is not harmed and can be used repeatedly.

Tip: This technique can be done using two different glitters or embossing powders in place of the beads. Most double-sided adhesive sheets are embossable because they are heat-resistant.

Die-cuts, such as this "love" shape, are a wonderful option. Die-cut machines are available for use at most art and craft and scrapbook stores and are generally free for use if you purchase the paper with them. The "Love" die-cut was cut from a double-sided heat-resistant adhesive sheet.

By using two different mediums, such as glitter and beads, a textural effect is created. The beads will raise up above the glitter. You may also want to experiment with different mediums such as two different colored glitters, embossing powders, or fine textural products such as decorative sand.

On this card the feather background and text was embossed. The heart was cut from a double-sided heat-resistant adhesive sheet, using a die-cut machine.

Embossing with White Powder & Chalks

Supplies

Antistatic pad

Assorted soft chalks

Black (or dark) matte card

Heat gun

Heat-set, pigment, or
    embossing ink pad

Rubber stamp

Sponge-tipped applicator

Spray sealant

White embossing powder

Option: Water-based markers

Even fine details stand out with this method. The white embossed areas accept chalk colors beautifully.

1. Apply antistatic pad to card surface.

2. Stamp image onto card with heat-set, pigment, or embossing ink.

3. Apply white embossing powder on card. Heat-emboss card, using heat gun.

4. Apply chalk on embossed surface, using applicator.

5. Option: Highlight selected areas over chalk with markers.

6. Spray card with fixative to retain sharpness.

Using chalks as a color medium provides a wide range of colors. This inventive technique has a different look than more traditional methods used for coloring stamped or embossed areas.

fact, it is quite easy.

Supplies

- 38-gauge aluminum
- Ball-tipped stylus
- Decorative hole punch
- Double-sided adhesive sheets or adhesive foam dots
- Permanent ink pad
- Rubber stamp
- Scissors
- Option: Meat tenderizing tool, pigment ink pad, alcohol inks

Heat from a heat gun may cause the art metal to change color. For example, when heated, copper will become somewhat pink. This effect can be desirable.

98

1. Stamp image onto aluminum with permanent ink. Let ink dry thoroughly, or speed it along with a heat gun.

2. Trace around the stamped image with small tip of stylus.

Note: This will make the design stand out and appear dimensional.

3. Cut around design, leaving metal border as desired.

4. Option: Tap metal surrounding design, using either ball-tipped stylus or meat tenderizer.

Note: This produces a hammered look.

5. Punch edges of metal with decorative hole punch.

Note: Scissors may also be used to create designs.

6. Adhere metal onto card with double-sided adhesive sheets or adhesive foam dots.

After stamping image with permanent ink and allowing it to dry, a mortise mask was used to expose only the stamped design. Lint-free cotton was used to daub colored alcohol inks into that area. The surrounding metal was hammered with a meat tenderizer and decorative punches were used around the edges.

Note: To make a mortise mask, stamp in the middle of a large sheet of paper. Cut out and discard stamped image for a reverse mask.

To achieve this embossed look, stamp metal with pigment ink to see the design. Trace image with stylus. Wipe away pigment ink (which will not adhere to metal), leaving just the outline of stamped image but no ink lines.

A meat tenderizer was used to texturize the stamped hair. A ball-tipped stylus was used on the back side to create a more raised texture The irregular edges were punched with a decorative hole punch. Lip color was added with a permanent marker.

Thick Embossing Enamel

This heavy-duty embossing enamel powder can create many different textures. The resin that creates this powder is larger than the average embossing powder. One application of thick embossing enamel creates a texture similar to linoleum tile. The powder appears to bead up and, once cooled, may be rubbed with rub-on metallic paste or pearlized powder for a metallic finish. Regular fine embossing powder will not produce this type of bumpy texture.

Supplies

Black matte card

Clear thick embossing enamel

Embossing, pigment, or heat-set ink pad

Heat gun

Option: rub-on metallic paste, pearlized dry pigment powder, soft cloth

Clear thick embossing powder was applied to this card for a wet, glossy look.

1. Holding embossing, pigment, or heat-set ink pad in hand, swipe ink across entire surface of card.

2. Apply embossing enamel on card. Heat-emboss card, using heat gun, until raindrop texture appears.

Note: Overheating will cause the powder to go smooth.

3. Option: Apply either rub-on metallic paste or pearlized dry pigment powder on surface. Buff with a soft cloth.

This technique works beautifully with other techniques. Pearlized pigment powder was added to the background of this card. Rub-on metallic paste helps enhance the color of this piece.

Thick embossing enamel was applied around this stamped pot image and adhered onto the background. Rub-on metallic paint was applied on the surface of the background card over a layer of thick embossing enamel.

Thick embossing enamel may be applied to many different surfaces. This photo frame and easel were first coated with black heat-set ink applied directly from the ink pad. Three layers of black embossing enamel were applied and heated. The embossing enamel was not allowed to cool until the third layer. While the third layer was molten, it was stamped. After the enamel was cool, rub-on metallic paste was applied to the surface.

This papier maché mask was embossed using several colors of thick embossing enamel all mixed together. Heat-set ink was applied from pad directly to mask. Powder was kept molten as non-melting embellishments were sprinkled in and stamp was pressed onto surface.

Note: Powder can be melted a section at a time or all at once in a (dedicated) toaster oven.

Custom-made jewelry like this can be made easily. Black heat-set ink and black thick embossing enamel was applied to cardboard shapes. The thick embossing enamel was then heated until molten and then stamped. Rub-on metallic paste was applied to the raised areas and dry pigment powder was rubbed into the crevices. Decorative paper and a pin back were adhered onto the back with double-sided adhesive tape.

Jewelry squares may also be made into mini accordion books. For each mini book, two squares were made as described above without the pin back. These were used for the front and back covers of the book. An awl was used to punch holes into the left side of the front cover and the right side of the back cover. The front and back covers were then "bound" with various materials such as wire, jute, and yarn. A long piece of decorative paper with a width slightly less than the covers was cut, stamped, and folded as shown. One end of the paper was then adhered onto the inside of the back cover.

106

Cracking with Thick Embossing Enamel

Two or more layers of thick embossing powder, when applied to a card, can be cracked to create an aged look.

Supplies

Archival or heat-set ink pad

Any color, any finish card for mounting

Any color matte card for stamping

Clear embossing ink pad

Clear thick embossing enamel

Double-sided adhesive sheet

Black or brown dye ink in refill bottle

Heat gun

Rubber stamp

Soft cloth or paper towel

Applying black dye ink to the surface of this cracked card gives it an aged appearance.

1. Stamp image onto card with archival or heat-set ink. Let dry.

2. Holding clear embossing ink pad in hand, swipe ink across entire surface of card.

3. Apply embossing enamel to card. Heat-emboss card, using heat gun, until melted. Keep warm and repeat this step a total of three times. Let cool.

4. When card is completely cooled it will curl. Carefully flatten the cooled card.

Note: The layers of embossing enamel will begin to crack.

5. Rub dye ink onto card with either refill bottle, paper towel, or dye ink pad as in Step 2 and let it seep into cracks. Remove excess ink with soft cloth or paper towels.

6. Adhere cracked card onto mounting card with double-sided adhesive sheet to give card stability and prevent further unwanted cracking.

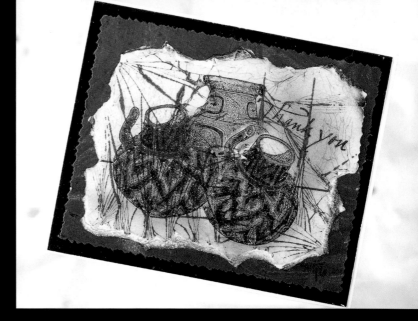

Above: Some of the dye that seeps through may bleed into the paper as in this example.

Below: Thick embossing enamel creates a smooth finish that is similar to hard plastic.

Thick Embossing Enamel on Metal

When you apply only one layer, thick embossing enamel can make metal appear hammered, but when multiple layers are applied, you may stamp into it, such as on page 110. Here are some decorative ways to turn ordinary metal objects into pieces for home decor.

such as on page 110

Supplies

Anything with a metal finish, such as a notebook with a metal cover, or a bandage tin

Any color thick embossing enamel

Heat gun

Heat-set ink pad

Soft rubber brayer

You would be surprised how easily your household items can become "objects d'art". It can be a fun experience in recycling.

Holding heat-set ink pad in hand, swipe ink across entire surface of metal.

Apply embossing enamel to metal. Heat-emboss, using heat gun. Apply more than one layer as desired.

On last hot layer of enamel, press inked stamp into enamel.

Other embellishments be added while enamel t.

What a great gift and a unique way to take notes. But remember, metal is not a porous surface and enamel can crack off if mishandled.

Thick Embossing Enamel & Shrink Plastic

Incorporate the art of shrink plastic with your cards and books. Unique and traditional shapes can be combined with rubber stamps to create collagible pieces of art. Because your image is stamped after the plastic shrinks, the image remains full size.

Supplies

Any color shrink plastic

Double-sided adhesive sheet or foam mounting tape

Fine-grit sandpaper

Heat gun or toaster oven

Heat-set ink pad

Rubber stamp

Scissors

Thick embossing enamel

Option: Rub-on metallic paste and/or dry pigment powder

This abstract shape is actually shrink plastic. Beaded embellishments surround this unusual shape, cut by hand. The exciting thing about this technique is that only the plastic shrinks, not the image. Sound impossible? We will explain how.

1. Cut a piece of shrink plastic to desired size and shape. Roughen the surface with sandpaper.

Note: ¼ of a full sheet is all that is needed.

2. Ink stamp with heat-set ink and set aside.

Note: Inked stamp will be used immediately after shrinking process is complete.

3. Holding heat-set ink pad in hand, swipe ink across entire surface of plastic.

Note: Pigment ink will not work for this technique.

4. Apply embossing enamel to plastic. Heat, using heat gun or toaster oven, until plastic shrinks and enamel is molten.

5. After shrinking process is complete, quickly and firmly stamp into the molten embossing enamel. Let cool.

Note: This pressing action forces the plastic into an unusual nugget shape, making it a wonderful embellishment for cards.

6. Option: Apply rub-on metallic paste or dry pigment powder to cooled surface of plastic.

7. Adhere plastic project onto card with double-sided adhesive sheet or adhesive foam dots.

Above: Rub-on metallic paste and glitter glue were added to the stamped image to give it sparkling highlights.

Left: Any shape can be traced, cut, and shrunk. You can also make and wear this as jewelry.

112

Supplies

Any color, any finish card for mounting

Any color embossing powder

Any color heat-set ink

Assorted colored thick or thin rubber shelf liner

Double-sided heat-resistant adhesive sheets

Heat gun

Rubber stamp

Scissors

Thick embossing enamel

Here, rubber shelf liner was embossed and used as background "paper". The add-on embellishments, even the leaves, were also embossed with thick embossing enamel. The center image was done on card stock and the words were stamped into shrink plastic.

1. Cut a piece of shelf liner and double-sided heat-resistant adhesive sheet to desired size and shape.

2. Peel protective liner from one side of adhesive sheet and adhere to one side of shelf liner.

3. Remove remaining protective liner from adhesive sheet and adhere to card as desired.

4. Holding heat-set ink pad in hand, swipe ink across entire surface of shelf liner, being careful not to get ink on card.

5. Apply embossing powder to shelf liner. Heat-emboss, using heat gun.

Tip: Embellishments may be added while shelf liner is being heated.

6. While shelf liner is hot, press inked stamp into surface.

Note: Let shelf liner cool before removing stamp.

Above and right: These butterflies and hearts were cut from shelf liner, using a die-cutting machine.

White shelf liner can become any color you like by using clear thick embossing enamel over colored heat-set ink.

The rubber shelf liner comes in many textures. This is a wavy texture rather than the burlap look on page 114.

dance to the music in your soul

Two layers of rubber shelf liner are used here. The thinner shelf liner makes a lacy background "paper." The thicker shelf liner may be stamped into.

Combining techniques can have beautiful results. The bottom layer of this card uses the Marbled Metallic Markers technique on page 50. The middle layer is embossed on black card stock. The top layer of rubber shelf liner was cut, using a die-cut machine, before it was heated and stamped.

Pearlized Fabric Paint

Supplies

Archival or dye ink
Black matte card
Pearlized fabric paint
Rainbow dye ink pad
Soft rubber brayer
Option: Rubber stamp

A thin layer of pearlized fabric paint was sponged on the surface, giving it texture. After it dried, dragonflies were stamped and embossed onto the surface.

1. Brayer card with rainbow dye ink.

Note: The color will not be seen on card.

2. Squeeze pearlized fabric paint onto one side of card and fold in half with paint on inside.

Note: This will create a "Rorschach" type of design when opened. The pearl paint will absorb the hidden color of dye ink.

3. Open card to reveal design as seen below.

4. Option: Stamp image onto separate card and adhere to background with adhesive foam dots.

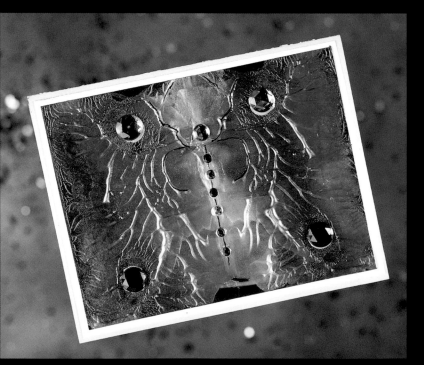

Above: This sponged-on texture is just one of many ways to apply pearlized fabric paint. The image of the eagle was stamped separately and adhered with adhesive foam dots.

Left: Here, the "Rorschach" type of design mentioned above is shown. This design resembles a butterfly. Embellishments were added while paint was still wet and tacky.

Right: Do not be afraid to use your fingers to create designs and patterns by pressing them into wet pearlized fabric paint. Decorative-edged scissors were used to create a unique border.

Below left and right: These two square designs combined pearlized fabric paint with glitter glue, and holeless beads to fill in the triangular stamped design areas. The result resembles floor tile.

Supplies

Candle

Matches

Rubber stamp with
  good detail

Spray fixative

White glossy card

Talk about accentuating the negative... The soot from an ordinary household candle provided the background for this beautiful Asian image.

1. Light candle. Hold card above flame with glossy side down.

Note: Be careful not to allow card to touch the wax, only the flame. Soot will begin to accumulate almost immediately.

2. Continue holding flame to card until an even film fills a large area of card.

Tip: For an artistic effect, burn the edges of the card.

3. Stamp soot with uninked rubber stamp.

Note: Image will appear like a negative.

4. Spray card with fixative, from 12" away, to avoid spots. Spray-sealing prevents soot from rubbing off.

Above: After this character for "serenity" was spray-sealed, the card stock was torn to create added interest. Embellishments were adhered to finish the look.

Right: Three muses come alive on this soot background. Glitter glue was used to hold the glass beads in place.

Artists' Gallery

Marg Hjelmstad

Marg Hjelmstad, a free-lance artist, discovered rubber stamps in 1981 and has incorporated them into her work ever since. Her interest in art already had expression in drawing, watercolors, and sculpture during her "earlier days" both in and out of school. In the late 1970s, while sitting in on graduate art classes at the University of Colorado in Boulder, Marg was invited to show her watercolor works in several juried shows.

She now teaches rubber stamping at *Stamp Cabana* stores in Florida and at other stores and conventions around the country. With years of stamping and a lifetime of working on artistic crafts and creations, this talented artist has learned techniques and developed methods to make marvelous cards and papercraft art.

Audrey Freedman

Audrey Freedman has been a rubber stamper since 1977. In 1990, she quit a position at CBS television to open *Stamp Oasis,* a retail store and internationally sold rubber stamp line, based in Las Vegas, Nevada.

"I am always amazed at how the use of rubber stamps creatively challenges me," she said. Audrey feels that by learning new things, she grows as an artist and a person, but feels grateful she is not starting out as a rubber stamper now. "There is so much these days to learn!"

Diane W. Lewis

Diane Lewis, a stamp artist from Plano, Texas, works in various mediums from paper to fabric to clay. She has made many samples for product manufacturers and stamp companies. She also teaches workshops.

Her artwork and written articles have been featured in many publications, including *Somerset Studio*, *RubberStampMadness*, *Rubber Stamper*, and *Stampington Book of Inspirations*. She was a featured artist in *Stampers Sampler* and the *Stamp Art Book* by Sharilyn Miller, and a cover artist for *Rubber Stampin' Retailer*.

Maria Dovellos

Maria Dovellos has been creating with rubber stamps for eight years. She and her husband George live in Tarpon Springs, Florida, with their three children, Nicholas, Jim, and Leah. Together, Maria and George have owned and operated Dove Brush Manufacturing, Inc., since 1985.

Maria developed the Dove Blender and has spent the last few years teaching and demonstrating blending techniques at stamp stores and conventions across the country.

Product Acknowledgment List

We would like to offer our sincere appreciation of the valuable support given in this ever-changing industry of new ideas, concepts, designs, and products. Several projects shown in this publication were created with the outstanding and innovative products developed by:

Art Metal, Ultra Thick Embossing
Enamel, and Shrink Plastic by
Suze Weinberg Design Studio, Inc.
39 Old Bridge Drive
Howell, NJ 07731
732-364-3136
www.schmozewithsuze.com

Artwork on pages 44, 109 by
Malana Corn
c/o Creative Daze
3730 N. Camino Leamaria
Tuscon, AZ 85716
520-323-2131

Dove Blender by
Dove Brush Mfg. Inc.
1849 Oakmont Ave.
Tarpon Springs, FL 34689
800-334-3683

Die-cuts by
Ellison Craft & Design
25862 Commercentre Dr.
Lake Forest, CA 92630-8804
800-253-2238
www.ellison.com

Metallic Markers by
Marvy Markers, Le Plume Pens
Marvy/Uchida Corp.
1027 E. Burgrove St
Carson, CA 90746

Mrs. Grossman's Stickers
3810 Cypress Dr.
Petaluma, CA 949543
707-763-1700

Pearl-Ex Pigment Powders by
Rupert, Gibbon & Spider, Inc.
P.O. Box 425
Healdsburg, CA 95448
707-433-9577
www.jaquardproducts.com

Penscore Moldable Foam by
Clearsnap Inc.
P.O. Box 98
Anacortes, WA 98221
800-448-4862
www.clearsnap.com

Liquid Pearls, Archival Ink, and
Resist Ink by
Ranger Industries, Inc.
15 Park Road
Tinton Falls, NJ 07724
800-244-2211
www.rangerink.com

Rubber Shelf Liner by
KCH Industries
800-543-3530

Spectra Art Tissue by
Bemiss Jason Corp.
One Bemiss Way
P.O. Box 717
Shirley, MA 01464
508-425-6761

Spray Webbing by
Krylon
31500 Solon Rd.
Solon, OH 44139
216-498-2300

Stitch Witchery by
HTC Handler Textile Corp.
24 Empire Blvd.
Moonachie, N J 07074
877-448-2669
www.htc-handler.com

Tria Alcohol Ink by
Esselte Letraset Ltd.
Ashford, Kent, TN23 2FL UK
(44) 0233-624421
(c/o MacPhersons Distributors in
United States 800-289-9800)

Kaleidacolor Rainbow Dye Ink
Pads by
Tsukineko
15411 NE 95th St.
Redmond, WA 98052
800-769-6633
www.tsukineko.com

Stamp Company Acknowledgment List

Acey Duecy
page 67
P.O. Box 194
Ancram, NY 12502

All Night Media
pages 42, 80
P. O. Box 10607
San Raphael, CA 94912
800-782-6733
www.allnightmedia.com

American Art Stamp
pages 72, 83
3892 Del Amo Blvd., Ste. 701
Torrance, CA 90503
310-371-6593
www.americanartstamp.com

Arizona Stamps, too
page 26
P.O. Box 6338
Paris, TX 75461
903-737-9885

Artistic Stamp Exchange
page 76
3568 Peoria St., Unit 606
Aurora, CO 80010

A Stamp in the Hand
pages 16, 33, 44, 56, 62, 67, 78, 106, 112
20630 So. Leapwood Ave., Ste. B
Carson, CA 90746
310-329-8555
www.astampinthehand.com

Cathy Daulman/My Stamps (Austrailia)
pages 41, 51
mystamps@excite.com

Comotion
pages 44, 61, 65, 98, 100, 102
10 E. Broadway, Ste. 402
Tuscon, AZ 85701
800-225-4894
www.comotion.com

Dewey, Inkum & Howe
A Div. of Clearsnap, Inc.
pages 73, 101
P.O. Box 98
Anacortes, WA 98221
800-448-4862
www.clearsnap.com

Distinked Impressions
page 61
5606 Greendale Rd.
P.O. Box 9639
Richmond, VA 23228

Era Graphics
pages 71, 101
2476 Ottowa Way
San José, CA 95130
408-364-1124
www.eragraphics.com

Fred B. Mullett
pages 30, 53, 77, 78, 84, 99, 107
2707 59th SW, Ste. A
Seattle, WA 98116
206-932-9482
rbbrfish@compuserve.com

Gold Thrush Arts
pages 48, 49
P.O. Box 6174
San José, CA 95150

Indigo Ink
pages 35, 117
A Div. of Primary Source
P.O. Box 5748
Redwood City, CA 94063
800-546-5982

Inkadinkadoo
page 70
Woburn, Mass
www.inkadinkado.com

Intentions
page 34

Judi-Kins
pages 8, 37, 131
17803 So. Harvard Blvd.
Gardena, CA 90248
310-515-1115
www.judi-kins.com

Kandy Lippincott (hand carver)
page 106
Kandylip@aol.com

Krafty Lady (Austrailia)
page 52
Rear 9 Edgewood Road
Dandenong VIC 3175
Austrailia
(61) 3-9794-6064

Love You to Bits
page 70
c/o Primary Source
P.O. Box 5748
Redwood City, CA 94063
800-546-5982
lytb@best.com

Magenta
Pages 17, 75, 106
351 Blain
Mont-Saint-Hilaire
QC, Canada J3H 3B4

Make an Impression
page 54
317 NW Gilman Blvd. #16
Issaquah, WA 98027
425-557-9247

Moe Wubba
page 29
P.O. Box 1445
San Luis Obisbo, CA 91445
800-547-1663
moewubba@aol.com

Moon Rose
page 97
P.O. Box 833
Yaphank, NY 11980
516-549-0199

Northwoods
Page 55
841 Eagle Ridge Lane
Stillwater, MN 55082
651-430-2840

Old Island Stamp Company
page 121
109 Meyer Rd.
Salt Spring Island, B. C. Canada
V8K1XY
www.saltspring.com/oldisland/

Paper Parachute
page 52
P.O. Box 91385
Portland, OR 97385

Paula Best Stamps
pages 25, 82, 106
445 Las Coches Ct.
Morgan Hill, CA 95037
408-778-1018

Personal Stamp Exchange (PSX)
page 38
360 Sutton Place
Santa Rosa, CA 95407
800-782-6748
www.personalstampexchange.com

Posh Impressions
page 26
4708 Barranca Parkway
Irvine, CA 92714
800-421-7674
www.poshimpressions.com

Printworks
Page 61
12403-B Slauson Ave.
Whittier, CA 90606
562-696-4562

Rubber Monger
pages 89, 118
Box 1777
Snowflake, AZ 85937
520-536-5128
www.rubbermonger.com

Rubber Poet
pages 16, 45
P.O. Box 218
Rockville, UT 84763
435-772-3441
www.rubberpoet.com

Rubber Stampede
pages 9, 22, 37, 73, 76, 117
800-632-8386
www.rstampede.com

Rubbermoon
page 73
P.O. Box 3258
Hayden Lake, ID 83835
208-722-9772

Rubberstilskin
page 114
P. O. Box 60909
Sunnyvale, CA 94068
www.aol.com/nanstamps

Sonlight Stamps
page 82
125 Business Ctr. Dr., Ste. E
Corona, CA 91720
909-278-5656
www.sonlightstamps.com

Stamp Cabana
pages 48, 49, 65, 104, 108
352 Park Ave. S.
Winter Park, FL 32789
800-987-8267
www.stampcabana.com

Stamp Francisco
page 65
2525 California St.
San Francisco, CA 94115
415-775-3355

Stamp Out
pages 19, 57, 60

Stamp Out Cute
pages 14, 47, 73, 85, 96
7084 N. Cedar # 137
Fresno, CA 93720
559-323-7174

Stamp Oasis
pages 58, 63, 76
4750 W. Sahara Ave. Ste. 17
Las Vegas, NV 89102
800-234-8735
www.stampoasis.com

Stamp Zia
pages 23, 46, 81, 86, 103, 119
29205 Elm Island
Waterford, WI 53185
414-534-6039

Stampa Barbara
pages 3, 21, 26, 42, 91
19 W. Ortega
Santa Barbara, CA 93101
805-962-4077
www.stampabarbara.com

Stampa Rosa
pages 23, 34
60 Maxwell Ct.
Santa Rosa, CA 95401
800-554-5744
www.stamparosa.com

Stampacadabra
page 108
5091 N. Fresno St.
Fresno, CA 93710
559-227-7247

index